Contents

Electricity

Unusual electrical inventions

Electricity isn't used just to make lights work and kettles boil. Many wonderful and unusual inventions use it too.

The electrically heated jacket

In 1932, the traffic police in America had a problem. They had to stand outside for a long time in the cold weather. So, they made an electrically heated vest! There were points in the street where the police officers could connect their vests to make an electric circuit and warm themselves up.

The Baker electric car

In 1909, Walter Baker invented an electric car!

The car was powered by batteries and could travel for 160 kilometres at up to 40 kmph before it needed recharging.

Over 100 years later, electric cars are now common all over the world.

This is a Baker electric car.

Can you think of any advantages of an electric car?

The smart wheel for bikes

This recent invention makes cycling much easier! The rear wheel of a bicycle can be replaced by an electric wheel. This is good news for people who have to cycle up hills!

The electric wheel can travel at 40 kmph for about 80 km without recharging!

Make it!

Follow these instructions to make a switch.

To make a switch you will need:
- two split pins
- a metal paperclip
- a piece of card that measures 8 cm long and 4 cm wide
- a ruler.

1. Measure the paperclip and make two small holes near the middle of the card that are the length of the paperclip apart.

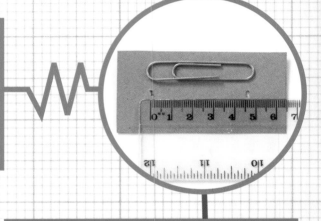

2. Push the split pins through the holes and splay the prongs on the reverse of the card to hold the pins in place.

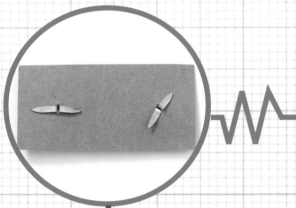

3. Hook one end of the paperclip over the top of one of the split pins. Check that the other end of the paperclip can be moved to touch the other split pin.

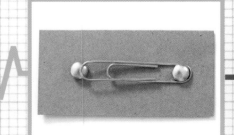

4. Collect a battery, three wires, a bulb and a *bulb* holder and construct a simple circuit that lights the *bulb*.

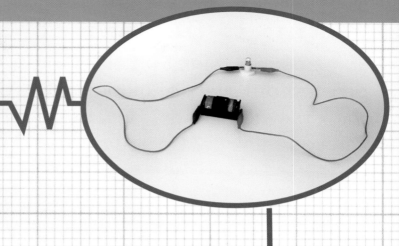

5. Disconnect a wire from the *bulb* holder and add an extra wire *so* that your split pin switch can *be* inserted.

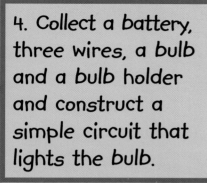

6. Connect the switch to the circuit by attaching the crocodile clips to the top of the split pins. Now open and close the switch by moving the paperclip.

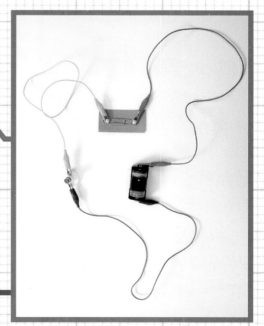

What happens to the *bulb*?

Taking it further

Some people think that electricity is the greatest discovery of all time. Why do you think they think that? How many reasons can you think of? Do you agree?

Humphry Davy

Humphry Davy's 'electric egg' lamp

Fascinating facts!

The first electric light bulb was made in 1800 by an English scientist called Humphry Davy.

If you had lived 100 years ago, your toast wouldn't have automatically popped up when it was ready. The first automatic pop-up toaster wasn't invented until 1919!

This toaster only toasted one side of the bread at a time. People had to turn the bread over themselves!

Dangers to Living Things

How do they know that?

If you want to know what an animal eats, you look it up. But how do scientists find out what an animal like a wild tiger eats in the first place? Tigers live in remote places and are very difficult to find and track. How could you find out what they eat?

What kind of things do you think this tiger would eat?

Bruiser is a Labrador like this dog.

Introducing Bruiser

Bruiser is a special dog. He is trained to smell out the scats of tigers and jaguars. When Bruiser has found a scat belonging to a tiger, he sits down to tell his owner he has found something.

Did you know?

Scat is another word for 'poo'. Scientists look through animals' poo to find hair and bones. This tells them what the animals have been eating.

Find out

Can you find any other ways that scientists find out what wild animals eat?

Food chains and humans

It's not just plants and wild animals that are part of food chains. We are part of food chains too. Humans are animals. Humans are also omnivores. We can eat both plants and animals.

Here are some food chains with a human at the top.

Some people eat meat from animals. Some people are vegetarian. This means that they do not eat meat that comes from an animal. How long will their food chains be?

Did you know?

Plankton is the name for tiny plants and tiny animals that float about in the sea. Plankton is so small that it can only be seen with a microscope.

Did you know?

There are two types of plankton – phytoplankton and zooplankton. Can you work out which one is the animal plankton from looking at its name?

Things to do

What is the longest food chain you can find with a human at the top? Can you beat four links?

Did you know?

There are masses and masses of plankton in the sea. The tiny plankton is all that some very large animals like whales eat.

Plan it!

Some children wanted to find out how putting a piece of old carpet on a patch of ground for two weeks would change the things that lived on that patch of ground.

The children all had different ideas about what to do.

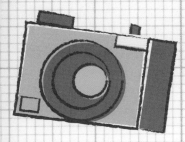

I'm going to look for living things when we lift the carpet up. I'll take photos too.

I'll make a sign that says 'Science Experiment' so that no-one will move the carpet.

I'm going to record which plants and animals I find on the ground before and after we put the carpet down.

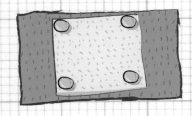

I'm going to put some stones around the edge of the carpet so that it doesn't blow away.

Things to do
Discuss the children's ideas and make a great plan of your own!

Human Nutrition

Your food's fascinating journey

Does your food look the same when it comes out as it did when it went in? Of course not! Let's explore how it changes.

Oesophagus: When you swallow, food travels down the oesophagus and into the stomach.

Mouth: Your food's journey starts here. Food is broken down into small pieces mixed with saliva.

Stomach: The stomach is a bit like the body's cement mixer. Strong muscular walls churn up food and mix it with stomach acids.

Rectum: The waste is stored here until we are ready to go to the loo.

Small intestine: Your food is now a liquid sludge mixed with substances from the liver and pancreas. Most of the useful nutrients in food go from your small intestine into your blood. Your blood takes the nutrients all around your body.

Large intestine: This is a two metre long tube where waste material from digestion is collected ready for excretion.

Types of teeth

When you were born, you didn't have any teeth. Your first teeth are called milk teeth. You have 20 of these. As you grow, you lose your first teeth and your permanent teeth grow through. You have 32 of these teeth.

Find out

Why is it so important to look after your teeth and gums?

Different shapes for different jobs

We have four different types of teeth in our mouths. They have different names and jobs. Next time you eat a meal think about the shape of the tooth and what makes it good for the job that it is doing.

Incisors cut our food. Canines are our 'fangs' and they grip and tear our food. Molars and pre-molars are used for chewing, crushing and grinding up food so that we can swallow it.

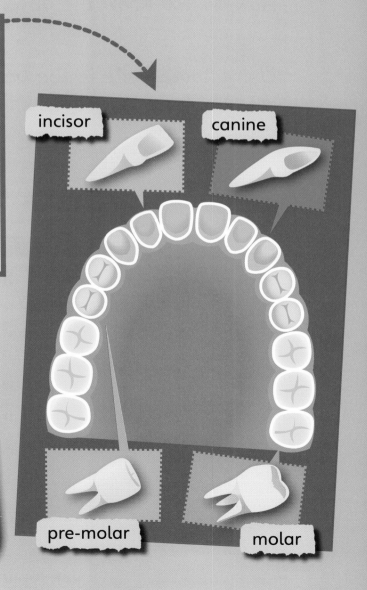

incisor

canine

pre-molar

molar

Did you know?

What can the shape of animals' teeth tell you about what they eat?

Decide it!

A fact is something that we can demonstrate to be true using evidence. An opinion is our belief or feeling about something.

Can you sort out the facts from the opinions? How do you know the difference?

Using toothpaste is the best way to clean your teeth.

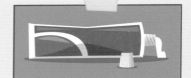

Plaque bacteria are always on your teeth.

Soft drinks are bad for your teeth.

You don't need to look after your milk teeth because you'll lose them anyway.

Acid from plaque bacteria causes cavities.

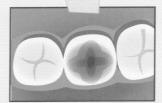

Sound

Vibrating air

Have you ever heard the sound of a bee buzzing as it flies? Bees flap their wings very quickly, vibrating the air as they move. The vibrations of the wings and the air make the buzzing sound.

Did you know?

Honey bees flap their wings 230 times each second!

When a guitar string is plucked it vibrates. This means that it moves backwards and forwards very quickly. This movement makes the particles of air next to the string vibrate too. The air carries the vibrations to our ears and then we hear the sound.

Measuring sounds

Sounds can be loud or quiet. The loudness of a sound is measured in decibels (dB). We call how loud a sound is its volume.

Big vibrations make loud sounds. Small vibrations make quieter sounds. The vibrations of this pneumatic drill produce sounds that are loud enough to damage human hearing. Workers in very loud environments need to wear sound-absorbing ear defenders to protect their hearing.

Things to do

What is the quietest sound you can hear? What is the loudest?

Did you know?

'Decibel' is named after Alexander Graham Bell. He invented the telephone!

High and low sounds

Every sound has a frequency. The frequency of a sound is the number of vibrations made in one second. This determines how high or low a sound is. We call this the pitch of a sound.

A referee's whistle makes very fast vibrations so it produces a very high-pitched sound.

A double bass makes lower-pitched sounds than a whistle. The vibrations it makes are slow so it produces a low sound.

Changing sounds

Look at this picture of instruments in an orchestra. They all sound different. How are the sounds made? How can the musicians change the sounds of their instruments? What can they do to alter the volume and pitch of a note?

Sensing sounds

All mammals, like us, have ears. We use our ears to detect sounds. Some animals have huge ears which are very sensitive and collect a lot of sounds.

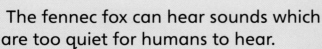

Dolphins use sound echoes to find their way around.

The fennec fox can hear sounds which are too quiet for humans to hear.

Did you know?

An echo happens when a sound wave bounces off objects and returns to our ears a moment after the original sound.

Find out

Find out how bats use sound to find their way around.

Secret sounds

Some sound is too high-pitched for humans to hear. We call this ultrasound. Doctors send waves of ultrasound into a body. The sound bounces off our organs and can create a picture of what is inside us.

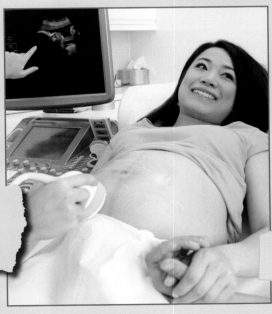

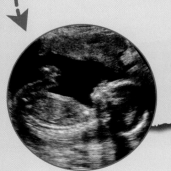

We can see a baby growing before it is born using ultrasound.

Grouping Living Things

What's out there?

Here are some photographs of living things that you might see near your school.

creeping buttercup

bird's foot trefoil

blue tit

ant

millipede

garden snail

white clover

centipede

woodlouse

robin

blackbird

Which of these living things have you seen?

Things to do

Some of these living things don't have labels. Can you find out what they are?

Did you know?

The most common bird in the UK is the wren. They are small and shy. We don't see them as often as other birds.

Compare it!

Weather in the Shetland Isles
Yearly rainfall: 1191mm
Average temperature: 7 °C
Wind: very strong winds

silver weed

sea rocket

green lizard

palm tree

jersey orchid

grass snake

otter

Weather in the Channel Isles
Yearly rainfall: 797mm
Average temperature: 12 °C
Wind: medium to strong winds

jersey lily

highland cattle

grey seal

jersey cow

Things to do

Work out which of these things live in the Shetland Isles and which live in the Channel Isles. Compare them to the living things near your school. Are they different? Why?

sea sandwort

I've found a new species

Sometimes scientists discover new species. Often they go far away to find them. One scientist found a new species of animal up his nose!

Tony Goldberg is a scientist. He knows all about ticks. When he came back from a trip to Africa, his nose was very sore. He pulled out a tick! He was amazed because it was a brand new species of tick.

Did you know?

Ticks have eight legs like spiders and mites. They feed on blood.

Things to do
Find out about other newly-discovered species.

Changes of State

Solid, liquid or gas?

Look around your classroom. How many different materials can you name? Everything around us is made of 'matter' – that's the scientific word for 'stuff'. The air we breathe is matter even though we can't see it. Scientists group matter into three types: solids, liquids and gases. We call these 'states'.

A 'property' describes something about a material. For example, steel is hard.

Did you know?

Solids have fixed shapes, but liquids and gases do not.

Which properties describe these materials? Are they solid, liquid or gas?

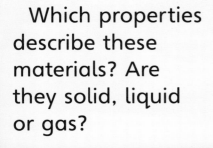  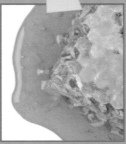 

Measure it!

Heating and cooling materials can change their properties. Freezing (or solidifying) is when a liquid cools down enough to become a solid. When liquid water becomes very cold it turns into solid water. We call solid water 'ice'.

Did you know?

The Ice Hotel in Sweden is the world's biggest igloo! Made entirely of ice, it is re-built every year.

Melting is when a solid warms up enough to become a liquid. Solid chocolate can melt and turn to liquid in your hands!

We measure temperature using a thermometer. There are lots of different types of thermometer.

  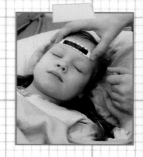 

Different materials change state at different temperatures. Look at these temperatures. Which of the materials below will melt at these temperatures?

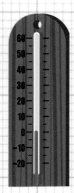 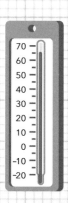 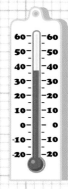  

Did you know?

Mercury is the only metal that is liquid at room temperature.

Water all around

On Earth we can find water in all three states – water, ice and water vapour. In nature, water is constantly changing state from liquid to gas and back again. We call this the water cycle.

Did you know?

How old is your water? You might think it is fresh from the tap but because water is constantly recycled, it's almost as old as Earth itself!

When a liquid changes to a gas, we call the process 'evaporation'.
When a gas cools and changes to a liquid, we call the process 'condensation'.

Find out

Find out why garden ponds often freeze in winter but the sea rarely does.

Did you know?

98% of the world's water is liquid. Less than 2% is ice.

The water cycle

In the water cycle, water is warmed by the Sun. It evaporates from the sea, rivers and lakes. It turns to vapour and rises in the air. Water vapour in the air becomes cold and changes back into a liquid forming clouds.

water vapour cools to make clouds

water condenses and falls as rain

water evaporates

sun warms water

As the clouds cool down, the water droplets join together to form rain. Rain falls on the land and eventually runs back into the sea. Then the cycle starts again!

Index